MOMENTUM

Momentum

©2014 Freedom Life
447 Noble Road, Christiana, PA 17509

Written by Sam Masteller | @sammylu
SamMasteller.com

ISBN: 978-0-9906744-0-5

MOMENTUM

*How to keep moving forward
when life seems stuck*

Sam Masteller

Momentum

INTRODUCTION

The Chinese Finger Trap

—

The brilliant Albert Einstein once said:

"I don't believe in combs."

(I kid, I kid. Although he must not have, right? Have you seen his hair?)

What he really said was:

"Insanity is doing the same thing over and over again and expecting different results."

We all have childhood memories of places we've gone on vacation, friends we've enjoyed hanging out with, and toys that provided countless hours of fun.

Some of my favorites included Nerf basketball, Atari, Operation, UNO, and G.I. Joe, to name a few. All of those toys were great, but looking back I can only think of one toy that I couldn't put down, not because it was fun, but because it was so frustrating!

The toy was called the Chinese finger trap, and if you've never played with one before, shame on your parents for depriving you!

The Chinese finger trap - pictured on the front of this book - is simple. You place one finger into either end of this oversized, woven tootsie roll and attempt to remove them. When you start to pull away you suddenly realize that you're trapped!

Funny how this little toy can cause a child, specifically yours truly, an irrational fear of having imprisoned, non-functioning fingers for the rest of his life.

The harder you pull back, the tighter the trap gets. And the tighter the trap gets the more you want to pull back! As a kid I experienced real moments of panic when I first started playing with this thing, wondering just what life would be like living with only eight fingers!

It was only a few years ago that I was studying for a message series on building holy momentum into your life when the Holy Spirit spoke to me in one of those oddly divine moments. I wasn't quite sure what a Far East-inspired party favor had to do with living a momentum filled life. Then it hit me:

Momentum is all about movement.

The only way to get free from the Chinese finger trap is the only way to get free from whatever may be holding you back.

You have to push forward.

You can't keep doing the same things over and over again and expect a different outcome. That's what Einstein called "insanity," remember?

This simple, yet powerful reminder was emblazoned in my heart in that moment, and it has stuck with me ever since.

Within the rest of the pages of this little book we'll explore what this idea means because I believe it can make a huge difference in your life.

If you want to experience the freedom and life only God can offer through your one and only life, keep pressing on and never give up!

Momentum

Chapter 1

Make Your Bed

"If you want to change the world, start off by making your bed."

- U.S. Navy Adm. William H. McCraven

—

Momentum is the art of movement.

The truth is, all of us have momentum in our lives, only for some it's negative momentum moving us in the wrong direction. God wants you moving forward into your destiny; He wants you to change the world.

In a speech given to the graduates at the University of Texas, Admiral McCraven, the commander of the U.S. Special Operations Command, shared a thought that

I believe can change your life today. It was an important lesson that he learned in his thirty-six years as a Navy SEAL:

"If you make your bed every morning, you will have accomplished the first task of the day," he said. "It will give you a small sense of pride, and it will encourage you to do another task, and another, and another. And by the end of the day that one task completed will have turned into many tasks completed."

"Making your bed will also reinforce the fact that the little things in life matter. If you can't do the little things right, you'll never be able to do the big things right. And if by chance you have a miserable day, you will come home to a bed that is made — that you made. And a made bed gives you encouragement that tomorrow will be better."

~

Momentum is all about the little things.

Yet many times in life we miss out on creating positive momentum because we overlook the little things. We want to get to tomorrow without living through today.

The Bible reminds us in Zechariah 4:10, *"Do not despise these small beginnings, for the LORD rejoices to see the work begin." (NLT)*

I've heard it said that your life moves at the *speed* of your decisions but success comes by the *quality* of your decisions.

One quality decision can turn the tide and help you move past whatever has you stuck today.

Decide today to do something new and move forward into the future that God has for you.

~

Momentum Declaration

Declare MOMENTUM over every area of your life today and repeat this in faith:

I will keep moving forward in faith! Nothing will hold me back from God's plans and purposes for my life!

Momentum

~

Momentum Verse

"... but I focus on this one thing: Forgetting the past and looking forward to what lies ahead, I press on to reach the end of the race and receive the heavenly prize for which God, through Christ Jesus, is calling us."

(Phillipians 3:12-14, NLT)

~

Momentum Thought

Focus forward and decide to do something new.

It's the little things that create positive momentum in life, so what's one thing you can do today to jump-start your life and move forward into your future?

Here are three ideas. Pick one and go for it.

And remember, momentum begins when you do something new!

Momentum

1. Organize ONE thing in your life today. (your room, your schedule, your home…)

2. Memorize ONE verse to build your faith.

3. Help ONE person that cannot repay you.

Journal

Momentum

Chapter 2

Beware of the Bear Dogs

"There is no better tool to conquer your fears than the act of moving forward."

- @ricklgodwin

—

There may have been more, but I remember three specific reasons why this particular summer morning in the mountains of Asheville, North Carolina was a beautiful one.

1. The weather was almost perfect.

2. We were on vacation visiting family and having a great time.

Momentum

3. My wife Michele and I were headed out for our morning walk to get some exercise and escape our children. Can I get an Amen?

(And yes, you are allowed to use phrases like "escape our children" when you have five young kids. It's in the U.S. Constitution.)

Despite feeling a little groggy as we began our stroll, I decided this would be the morning we'd take a new route, down a busy road, to check out a new housing development Michele wanted to see. Maybe I wanted to score some brownie points, maybe I just wanted some new scenery to get my mind off my burning thighs.

As we made our way along that busy route trying to wake up (at least I was), it seemed like an ordinary morning; that is until out of nowhere two mammoth dogs ran up an embankment right toward us.

Now, I'm not one to embellish details of a story, but I swear these things were nine feet tall and drooling at the mouth, ready to attack us. They may have even been shouting at us in Russian, but don't hold me to that.

What happened next is something I'm not proud of. Whether it was the early morning grogginess or the

Momentum

fact that these dogs were part grizzly, I don't know, but in that instant I lost any shred of bravado and manliness that I had. (Before you judge me, have you ever been surprise attacked by a bear dog? Didn't think so.)

I can't tell you how scared I was in those next few seconds. The only other time I've been that frightened was the time I woke up in the middle of the night to my son staring right into my face. That was absolutely terrifying. But not quite as terrifying as the prospect of being mauled to death by a bear dog.

Before I even realized what I was doing, I let out a string of unintelligible noises like a tween at a Beiber concert and I bolted from the bear dogs…directly into the middle of the busy road.

Fortunately for me, Michele wasn't nearly as groggy (or terrified) as I was. She grabbed my hand and pulled me back out of the way of the oncoming traffic before I became a human hood ornament.

Turned out the bear dogs weren't interested in eating me. (Also turns out they weren't nine feet tall or part bear either.) If not for Michele's quick thinking, I might have lost a game of real-life Frogger that morning.

Momentum

She grabbed my hand, we caught our breath, and then we kept moving forward.

~

It's amazing, the things fear can cause you to do.

It can cause you to stop dead in your tracks, it can force you to retreat to the comfort of where you were, and sometimes it can send you into oncoming traffic!

Running away from our present challenges will always cause us to be stuck in our past.

That morning I lost complete momentum from my run-in with the bear dogs. I didn't want to walk after that. Between the dogs and the cars, it was an unsettling and terrorizing moment.

The truth is, we all find ourselves in situations at some point in life where we are overcome with fear and don't know what to do or where to turn. It's so easy in these moments to let fear paralyze us or cause us to retreat.

In your life it's probably not a bear dog attack, but you can bank on the fact that fear will attack you in one of these five areas:

1. Spiritual Life
2. Emotional Life
3. Relational Life
4. Physical Life
5. Financial Life

Fear is the great exaggerator.

It lies and tells you that your future won't be any different than your past or present.

But here's what the Bible says in John 10:10:

"The thief does not come except to steal, and to kill, and to destroy. I (Jesus) have come that they may have life, and that they may have it more abundantly."

Right now, the enemy is attempting to steal your faith and momentum in one of those five areas.

Take a moment. Identify what it is. Be aware of the attack of the enemy and determine that you will not shrink back in fear, but you will keep moving forward.

Stare down that bear dog with the Word of God. You will not be defeated, you are moving on to all that God has for you.

Momentum

~

Momentum Declaration

Declare MOMENTUM over every area of your life today and repeat this in faith:

No weapon formed against me will prosper. I have a heritage of protection. I will keep moving forward in faith!

~

Momentum Verse

"No weapon formed against you shall prosper, and every tongue which rises against you in judgment you shall condemn. This is the heritage of the servants of the Lord, and their righteousness is from Me," says the Lord."

(Isaiah 54:17, NJKV)

~

Momentum Thought

Decide to move past your fear.

Flip back a page and consider that list one more time.

Which area of your life is being challenged by fear? Determine right now to ignore the lies and intimidation from the enemy (Satan) and move forward into your future today.

Write down the desired, faith-filled outcome of the challenge(s) that you are facing today.

Journal

_____
_____
_____
_____
_____
_____
_____
_____
_____
_____
_____
_____
_____
_____
_____

Momentum

Chapter 3

Overcoming Momentum Suckers

—

We've all heard the expression, "it sucked the life right out of me." Unless you've got a serious leech problem, that expression is usually reserved for draining people and difficult life situations we all encounter.

(If you do have a serious leech problem, put this book down and go get some help. We'll wait for you.)

Truth is, there are probably some people in your life you're thinking of right now that fit that bill; a co-worker, family member or someone you routinely avoid in Walmart.

Momentum

Life happens. Bad news arrives. Draining moments occur. If we are not careful, they can steal away the momentum-filled life that God has called us to.

It's in these moments that we have to cling to God's word. His word produces good things in our lives. It removes our limitations, empowers our faith, and keeps us moving forward; but we've got to keep it rooted in our hearts.

In Matthew 13 we find a powerful parable that teaches us to watch out for the momentum suckers because they limit our potential and our future.

Through the image of a sower and a seed, Jesus shows us how God's holy momentum can be sucked out of our lives.

Here's how Jesus explained the parable to his disciples:

"Now listen to the explanation of the parable about the farmer planting seeds: The seed that fell on the footpath represents those who hear the message about the Kingdom and don't understand it. Then the evil one comes and snatches away the seed that was planted in their hearts. The seed on the rocky soil represents those who hear the message and immediately receive it with joy. But since they don't have deep roots, they don't last long.

Momentum

They fall away as soon as they have problems or are persecuted for believing God's word. The seed that fell among the thorns represents those who hear God's word, but all too quickly the message is crowded out by the worries of this life and the lure of wealth, so no fruit is produced."

(Matthew 13, NLT)

Jesus taught us about four different momentum suckers that threaten to limit the expansive lives God has called us to. These momentum suckers attack the five areas of our lives we looked at in the last chapter:

Momentum Sucker #1
A Lack of Understanding (v. 19)

Momentum Sucker #2
Persecution and Problems (vv. 20-21)

Momentum Sucker #3
The Worries of Life (v. 22)

Momentum Sucker #4
A Love of Money (vv. 22)

Take a good look at that list. Be honest and ask yourself if you're facing any of these today.

Momentum

The seed of God's Word in your life is powerful and transformative. It will give birth to every good thing God has planned for you.

The enemy will attempt to use momentum suckers in your life to keep you stuck.

His goal is to limit you by keeping you in defeat and discouragement.

When that happens, simply declare and hold fast to the promises of God.

~

Momentum Declaration

Declare MOMENTUM over every area of your life today and repeat this in faith:

I will keep moving forward into God's plan for my life. I will not be limited by the devil. I will not give into temptation. I will keep moving forward in faith!

~

Momentum Verse

"So give yourselves completely to God. Stand against the devil, and the devil will run from you. Come near to God, and God will come near to you. You sinners, clean sin out of your lives. You who are trying to follow God and the world at the same time, make your thinking pure."

(James 4:7-8, NCV)

~

Momentum Thought

Refuse to be limited by your circumstances.

Make a list of the circumstances in your life that you sometimes feel limited by. Try to come up with at least three to five things.

Spend some time in prayer asking God to give you faith to not see these circumstances as limitations, but rather as opportunities for your faith to increase as He does amazing things through your life.

Momentum

Journal

Momentum

Momentum

Chapter 4

Take Your Next Step

"Your life does not get better by chance, it gets better by change."

- @drdavemartin

The famous architect Frank Lloyd Wright designed many beautiful buildings, homes, and other magnificent structures.

Toward the end of his career, a reporter asked him, "Of your many beautiful designs, which one is your favorite?" Without missing a beat, Frank Lloyd Wright answered, "My next one."

That incredible confidence and perspective is what is required to live a momentum-filled life.

The goal of the Christian life is not simply to arrive safely at our destination. God wants us to experience things that we've never even dreamed possible, things we can only do when we partner with Him.

There will be moments when you feel like your holy momentum has been sucked away.

In those moments you need to go for a walk.

No, not the kind of walk where bear dogs scare you into oncoming traffic. I'm talking about the kind of walk that the Apostle Peter took one stormy night on the Sea of Galilee.

Matthew 14 says Peter was with the disciples on a boat in the midst of a storm. After struggling for hours with the elements they were feeling frustrated, discouraged and scared.

Any momentum they had gathered after leaving the shore had been completely lost.

In that moment, Jesus did what he always does when we are stuck, hopeless, and full of fear. He came to them with an invitation.

Momentum

"But Jesus quickly spoke to them, 'Have courage! It is I. Do not be afraid.' Peter said, 'Lord, if it is really you, then command me to come to you on the water.' Jesus said, 'Come.' And Peter left the boat and walked on the water to Jesus."

(Matthew 14:27-29, NCV)

When we hear this passage we marvel at the fact that Peter walked on water, but the truth is Peter didn't walk on the water; he walked on the words of Jesus. Peter took Jesus at his word and took a step into the miraculous.

Many times we miss our momentum miracles because of the voices we listen to.

While Jesus is calling us forward in our faith, we all have many voices in our life calling for us to stay back.

According to Rick Warren, research indicates that most people speak at a rate of 150 to 200 words per minute, but the mind can listen to about 500-600 words a minute. That's why you can listen to someone and update Facebook at the same time.

What's even crazier? Our internal dialogue - the words that we say to ourselves - happens at a rate of 1,300 words per minute! How? Because our mind sees in pictures, and you can see a thought in a nano-second!

Put yourself in Peter's sandals for a moment and imagine the things you would be picturing and what you would be saying to yourself.

I know my internal dialogue would probably have been focused on NOT drowning…I honestly don't know if I would have let go of the boat!

But despite whatever voices he was hearing, Peter decided to only listen to Jesus' voice and take a step that forever changed his life. He refused to allow the limitations of who he was or his current circumstances to keep him from moving forward.

So what about you? Just like he invited Peter, Jesus still invites those who want to follow him to take steps that require faith.

When you decide by faith to tune into the voice of the LORD, momentum swings in your favor. In Peter's case, he did something only one other person had ever done before (Jesus); he walked on water!

Momentum

Some of you may be thinking, "Yeah, but Peter was a disciple chosen by God. I'm not on that level. I work at Panera Bread and drive an old Civic. I'm nobody!"

First of all, thanks for working at Panera, they make fantastic cinnamon crunch bagels. And second of all, you are NOT a nobody. You were handpicked by God to live in this exact time and place to do things for Him.

We can be so quick to disqualify ourselves from what God has qualified us for, when God is saying we have all that we need to do great things for Him.

The truth is, you are every bit as chosen to do good works for God as Peter was.

And what about those of you worried that you will take a step back and start sinking? Well, let's go back to the Chinese finger trap for a moment.

Remember: when you pull back you stay stuck, when you push forward you gain freedom.

The same goes with life. Every small step is a leap into your future. Hear Jesus calling you right now to take your next step!

~

Momentum Declaration

Declare MOMENTUM over every area of your life today and repeat this in faith:

I will take my next step in faith and receive all of God's promises for my life! I believe my best days are still in front of me so I will keep standing on God's promises.

~

Momentum Verse

"For we are His workmanship, created in Christ Jesus for good works, which God prepared beforehand so that we would walk in them."

(Ephesians 2:10, NASB)

~

Momentum Thought

Ignore the negative voices that can keep you from your destiny and choose to take your next step.

What do you need to stop saying to yourself?

What voices do you need to tune out of your heart and mind?

Journal

_____
_____
_____
_____
_____
_____
_____
_____
_____
_____
_____
_____

Momentum

Chapter 5

Keep Moving Forward

"If you can't fly then run, if you can't run then walk, if you can't walk then crawl. But whatever you do, you have to keep moving forward."

- Martin Luther King, Jr.

—

You know that feeling you have when you're about to enjoy an amazing vacation? I was drenched in it.

It was a beautiful day in Baltimore, Maryland and my wife and I were getting ready to set sail on a cruise headed for glorious Bermuda.

Just a few weeks earlier, in front of our whole church family, we were surprised by our gracious staff with this generous gift. We don't travel very often away from our five kids because, well, no one really wants to watch your kids when you have five of them! True story.

I guilted — I mean asked — my mother-in-law to take some time off of work and fly in for a few days so that we could go away, and amazingly she said 'Yes'.

This was our first time on a cruise so we arrived early to get acclimated and take some pictures for the kids. The last thing we wanted was drama or hiccups.

If you've never been on a cruise, boarding one is similar to boarding an airplane. If you are going out of the country, you need a passport or birth certificate.

I repeat, you need to have your passport or BIRTH CERTIFICATE. (Yes, this is an important detail.)

The fine gentleman at the check-in counter took our tickets and bags and welcomed us to the cruise, but he singled me out and asked me to step forward to speak to a representative of the cruise line.

Clueless as to what was going on I happily stepped forward. Maybe I was the one millionth customer and was going to get VIP treatment all week?

Not so much.

Momentum

The kind female representative looked at me and started off by saying, "We really want you to go on the cruise today sir." Uh oh. It was in that moment I realized something must be wrong.

Did I have my ticket? Yup. Was I carrying any weapons or explosives on me? Nope. I was stumped. Maybe they were worried about me dying of sunburn because my skin was so white? At this point, anything was possible.

"To go on this cruise today," she continued, "you will need a birth certificate or a passport."

"No problem," I told her, "I already gave my birth certificate to the check-in guy."

"Sir, what you have is a birth registration, not a birth certificate," she said.

In my heart, I was sure that she was wrong. My mother had given me my birth document and my mom is like Mother Theresa; I knew she wouldn't lead me astray. I had used it for identification purposes my entire life. Surely this was a mistake.

Despite my insistence that we had the proper documentation, she escorted Michele and I to another area with a dozen or so other people to help us come up with a solution to our problem; a location I now refer to as "Cruise Ship Purgatory."

Everyone in Cruise Ship Purgatory can see the happy passengers boarding the boat, but no one there can do anything to join them. It is a terrible place.

Desperate, I asked the lady what we needed to do to be able to board the cruise. I knew the cruise was non-refundable. I also knew that to get someone to watch my five kids for a week was more difficult than an Act of Congress.

I looked at Michele and said, "Start praying and keep believing. We are going on that cruise."

In that moment, the Holy Spirit reminded me of Psalm 84:11, *"For the LORD God is our sun and our shield. He gives us grace and glory. The LORD will withhold no good thing from those who do what is right." (NLT)*

My wife looked fearful. I *felt* fearful. But God gave me a word that favor was already released into my future and I was not going to give up.

I took a deep breath and turned to the cruise employee, who informed us she would help in any way that she could to ensure that we made it on the ship.

(And by "help in any way," she meant "you can use my fax machine while I sit over here and work on my cuticles. Good luck.")

It was 1:45 p.m. We had until 3:15 p.m. at the absolute latest to get a copy of my birth certificate. Ninety minutes. No problem! Right?

"Mom, I need you to prove that I'm your son," I said on the phone trying my best to be jovial and full of faith. After I explained the situation, she went to check her papers for my birth certificate. "Problem solved," I thought.

"You know son, it's funny," she said getting back on the phone. "I have both of your sisters' birth certificates, but I only have what I already gave you." Swing and a miss.

I turned to the lady assisting us and asked what I should do since apparently I was adopted or kidnapped as a child. She encouraged me to call vital statistics in my state, which happened to be the Florida of the north, also known as Pennsylvania.

With my wife by my side and God's Word in my heart, I went on my smartphone, found the number, and made the call. A nice person on the other end of the line answered and said, "How can I help you?"

"My name is Sam," I said. "I pastor a great church in the middle of nowhere called Freedom Life. My staff gave me tickets for this amazing cruise that I'm trying to board. I have five kids that are taken care of for the week. I need a vacation badly and I really would like to go on the cruise. All I need is a copy of my birth certificate, can you help?"

"Absolutely," she replied. I breathed a sigh of relief. "Just drive on over and we will fast track you through our process and get you on your way."

Turns out there are strict government regulations about faxing birth certificates and she couldn't do it for me. If I couldn't go get it, it would have to be a family member.

No one in my immediate family, including me, was within two hours of Harrisburg and it was now after 2:00 p.m. I needed a miracle.

In that moment, I made an important decision.

Momentum

I decided to keep moving forward. Even stuck there in Cruise Ship Purgatory I knew if we could just get some Holy Momentum we could still make it on time.

I asked the woman on the phone if I could speak with her boss to which she politely agreed. When he came on the line I gave him the same story. "Hi, my name is Sam. I pastor a great church in the middle of nowhere called Freedom Life. I have five kids that I'm trying to escape from. I need to get on this cruise! Can you help me?"

"I'd love to help you," the kind man replied. "All you need to do is come in person to get your birth certificate…"

I again asked for someone else to talk to who might be able to help. Wash, rinse, repeat. Two more times and the answer hadn't changed.

"I need to keep moving forward," I kept telling myself.

"God withholds no good thing from those who do what is right. This cruise is a good thing, I need to go on this cruise!"

As I continued to keep making phone calls I also continued to keep moving around. It became increasingly difficult to hear due to the massive amount of grumbling, expletives and arguing coming from those who were stuck in Cruise Ship Purgatory with me.

Security had to be called in to help settle people down. They were angry, discouraged and frustrated. It wasn't exactly an encouraging environment. But every time negativity got close to me, I just kept moving away from it. Just because they weren't going to reach their destination didn't mean that I couldn't reach mine.

After speaking with half of the city of Harrisburg I was given the number for the Vital Statistics Office in New Castle, Pa. New Castle was even further away than Harrisburg, but I had nothing else to do, so I figured I would give it a shot and maybe even make a new friend. I knew I would probably get the same story as before, but I was determined to go down fighting.

I explained my situation to two more people, asking the same thing and getting the same response.

More swings, more misses. Strike fifteen!

I paused and decided to ask one more question before I gave up and accepted my fate as a permanent member of Cruise Ship Purgatory.

"What would you do," I asked, "if you were in my position?" Fortunately she didn't respond with, "bring your real birth certificate next time, moron!" or I may have committed a felony or three.

Instead I was asked, "Have you contacted your local representative?"

I had no idea who my representative was, so she gave me the phone number of her local representative.

It was 2:58 p.m.

This was my last shot. I placed the phone call to the local representative and a sweet grandmotherly woman answered.

"Hi, my name is Sam Masteller… I have a great church in the middle of nowhere… five kids…need this cruise… can you help me?!"

"Yes." she said.

"Okay, how?" I had been burned already by folks who thought they could help. I wasn't falling for it again.

She said she would be willing to take my name, personally purchase my birth certificate and fax it over to the cruise line for confirmation.

"When do you need it?" she asked.

"In fifteen minutes," I said, cringing. She laughed. Not a good sign.

She told me that it was pretty much impossible for her to run down the block to the Vital Statistics office and back in time to fax them, but she would try if I wanted her to.

Umm, yes please!

I faxed over my ID with the assistance of my cruise employee and waited.

Time was running out.

Everyone at the cruise line was amazed we had gotten this far and were all anticipating what was about to happen. I figured if I was going to be letdown, I might as well get my hopes all the way up!

At 3:14 p.m. I received a call from this angel by the name of Sarah. Out of breath she excitedly explained to me that when she arrived at Vital Statistics, they were anxious to help because they had already heard my story. They processed everything in record time and she was back at her office faxing my birth certificate as we were speaking.

As God as my witness, I glanced at the time when the fax came through.

It was exactly 3:15pm.

The workers for the cruise line said they had never seen anything like that happen before.

Michele and I grabbed our bags and boarded the ship for what turned out to be an amazing time in Bermuda. My heart was full, my faith was exploding and my legs were on fire from the stress of the last ninety minutes!

There were so many times I had wanted to give up, but I had a promise from God in my heart that he has good things for me.

Honestly, I still can't fully comprehend how everything came together.

What I do know is that God is gracious and if you quit too soon, you will never experience the miracle that God wants to do in and through your life.

No matter what, keep moving forward into God's great plan for you!

~

Momentum Declaration

Declare MOMENTUM over every area of your life today and repeat this in faith:

God has good things released into my future because I am His child. He is for me, so it doesn't matter what may come against me. I will keep moving forward in faith!

~

Momentum Verse

"For the LORD God is our sun and our shield. He gives us grace and glory. The LORD will withhold no good thing from those who do what is right."

(Psalm 84:11, NLT)

~
Momentum Thought

Determine to keep moving forward in faith.

What is one thing that you can do to jump-start your life and move forward into your future today?

Here are three ideas. Pick one and go for it.

Remember, momentum begins when you take action and do something new!

1. Write out your dreams using the journal space on the next page.

2. Find a Bible reading plan. (Try YouVersion.com)

3. Do something to invest into the important relationships in your life.

Journal

Momentum

Momentum

Momentum

How To Keep Moving Forward

1. Focus Forward And Do Something New

2. Decide To Move Past Your Fear

3. Refuse To Be Limited By Your Circumstances

4. Ignore The Negative Voices And Take Your Next Step

5. Determine To Keep Moving Forward In Faith

Momentum

Do You Know Jesus?

There is a big gap between us and God.

We are separated by sin, and no one is exempt. We need God to forgive us, restore us, and empower us in this life. Our only hope is through Jesus — he is the bridge across the chasm of sin to God.

Jesus is God's Son who came to earth and lived a perfect life. His death broke the curse of sin for all of mankind. Salvation is God's free gift to us; we don't have to earn it.

"For God so loved the world that he gave his one and only Son, that whoever believes in him shall not perish but have eternal life." John 3:16

Through Jesus we can be saved from the ugliness of this world, receive power for change, and anticipate eternity with our Heavenly Father who created us with purpose and loves us beyond comprehension.

How does someone receive salvation?

Surrender your life to Jesus through a prayer something like this:

Dear Jesus, I need you in my life. Today I choose to follow you. Thank you for the gift of salvation. I lay down my past and my former ways. Please forgive me of my sins and the pain I've caused to others, to myself, and to you. My slate is clean, and I'm beginning a new life with you as my guide. I put my trust in you. Help me to love you and to love others. Amen.

Once we are justified through faith, we can have peace with God (Romans 5:1).

If you have given your life to Jesus today, please send us an email at hope@freedomlife.tv to tell us about your commitment.

We would like to pray for you and offer you resources for growing in your relationship with Jesus and other Christ-followers.

You are no longer alone!

Made in the USA
Charleston, SC
27 November 2015